LANDSCAPES of LEGEND

CITIES OF SPLENDOUR

— ✦ The facts and the fables ✦ —

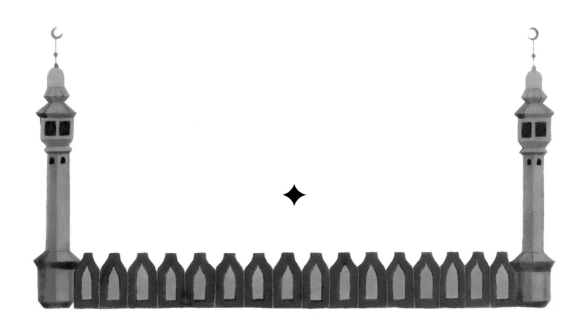

Finn Bevan
Illustrated by Diana Mayo

W
FRANKLIN WATTS
NEW YORK • LONDON • SYDNEY

First published in 1998 by Franklin Watts
96 Leonard Street, London EC2A 4RH

Franklin Watts Australia
14 Mars Road
Lane Cove
NSW 2066

Series editor: Rachel Cooke
Art director: Robert Walster
Designer: Mo Choy
Picture research: Sue Mennell

A CIP catalogue record for this book
is available from the British Library.

ISBN 0 7496 2955 X

Dewey Classification 398.2

Printed in Singapore

Picture acknowledgements:
AKG London/ Erich Lessing pp. 23, 26; James Davis Travel Photography p. 27;
Eye Ubiquitous p. 15r; Werner Forman Archive p. 10r; Robert Harding p. 14;
Hutchison Library p. 15l; Image Bank p. 6 (Alan Becker);
Ann and Bury Peerless pp. 19l, 19r; N. J. Saunders p. 10l

Contents

✦

The Story of Cities

Until about 12,000 years ago, people lived a nomadic lifestyle, wandering from place to place in search of food and pasture for their animals. Then they began to settle in one place all year round, to farm the land and build permanent houses and homes. From these first small villages grew the first towns and cities.

Sacred Cities

Some cities grew rich on trade. Others became the capitals of mighty empires and kingdoms. There are stories which tell of great events in a city's history, tales of battles and great deeds, festivals and fabulous buildings. These cities became the centres not only of people's daily lives but also their beliefs and religions.

Many myths and legends have grown up around the origins of great cities. They tell how the cities grew up on sacred sites chosen by the gods. The city of Athens in Ancient Greece was named after the goddess Athena, who gave the people the gift of a sacred olive tree. Some cities even became the gods' homes on Earth, with splendid shrines and temples built in their honour. For example, Varanasi in India is the god Shiva's earthly home.

The most sacred cities are those that have gained fame for a special event, such as the birth or death of a religious leader, a holy man or prophet. These include Mecca, in Saudi Arabia, the birthplace of Muhammad, and Bodh Gaya, in India, where the Buddha discovered the meaning of life. Like other sacred cities, these have become major places of pilgrimage to which people travel as an act of worship.

City of the Seven Hills

ITALY

Tiber

Rome •

Rome began as a small group of villages built on seven hills in central Italy, along the River Tiber. According to legend, Rome was founded in 753BCE. By the 1st century CE, it was the most important city in the western world – the magnificient capital of the vast Roman Empire. Rome is still one of the world's important cities, as the centre of the Roman Catholic Church and home to its leader, the Pope.

Vatican

Navona Square

RIVER TIBER

Farnese Palace

Roman Landmarks

Rome became a Christian city in the 4th century CE and Rome today reflects both its ancient and Christian heritage. Ruins such as the Colosseum and the Forum as well as churches form the city's landmarks. The Forum, or market place, was the centre of ancient Rome. People met there to talk business and politics in the Basilica Aemilia. The design of this building was adapted for the first Roman churches. Another landmark, the Pantheon, has changed little since it was built around 125CE as a temple to Mars and Venus. It was later used as a church.

The Colosseum amphitheatre as it stands today. Opened in 80CE, it seated about 50,000 spectators, who flocked there to watch gladiator fights and wild beast shows.

RIVER TIBER

Mausoleum
of Augustus

Trinità dei
Monti

Quirinal hill

Quirinale
Palace
and Square

Viminal hill

Pantheon

The Forum including
Basilica Aemilia

Santa Maria Maggiore

Capitoline
hill

Hut of Romulus

Esquiline hill

Santa Maria in
Cosmedin

Palatine hill

Colosseum

Caelian hill

Circus Maximus

Aventine
hill

Roman River Gods
Flowing through the centre of the city, the River Tiber provided a convenient route to the sea, some 24 km to the west. As sea trade grew, so did Rome's prosperity. So important was the river that the Romans worshipped it as a god, Tiberinus. In legend, Rhea Silvia, the mother of Romulus and Remus, became the Tiber's wife, when she was thrown into the river by her wicked uncle.

Romulus and Remus
Twin brothers Romulus and Remus were the legendary founders of Rome, and Romulus became its first king. Throughout the city, places associated with their lives were revered as sacred. They included the Lupercal Cave on the slopes of the Palatine Hill, where the boys were said to have been suckled by a she-wolf, and a wooden hut on the same hill, where Romulus is said to have lived.

The founding of Rome

This is the story of Romulus and Remus, and the founding of Rome.

◆

Long ago, two baby boys were born. They were twins, called Romulus and Remus, the sons of a priestess, Rhea Silvia, and Mars, the mighty god of war. Rhea's uncle, King Amulius, was furious when he heard the news. He was afraid that the children would seize his throne. So he had his niece thrown into the waters of the River Tiber. Then he put the babies into a basket and threw them in after her – they were sure to drown.

But the twins did not die. The basket drifted downstream and came to rest at the foot of the Palatine Hill. There, a kindly she-wolf heard the babies crying. She took them to her den, gave them nourishing milk to drink, and brought them up as if they were her own. A woodpecker also brought them food, for the wolf and the woodpecker were sacred to Mars, the boys' father.

When the boys were older, they went to live with a shepherd called Faustulus and his wife. They grew up to be healthy and strong. But they never forgot the she-wolf who saved their lives, and vowed to build a city in her honour. After many squabbles and quarrels, they chose a spot on the Palatine Hill, where they had been washed ashore.

But the quarrels continued – which twin should rule the new city? So Romulus went to the Palatine Hill, and Remus went to the Aventine Hill, and both of them waited for a sign. It soon came. Six vultures flew over the Aventine. But twelve flew over the Palatine. Romulus was to be king.

Romulus built a wall to defend his new city. Remus did not think much of it. He leapt right over the wall to show how useless it would be if an enemy attacked. But he didn't live to find out if he was right. In a terrible rage, Romulus drew his sword and killed his brother. And so Romulus ruled his new city alone and named it after himself: Rome – one of the greatest cities ever known.

The City in the Lake

USA

MEXICO

Mexico City •
(Tenochtitlan)

Today, the ancient city of Tenochtitlan lies buried under the modern buildings of Mexico City. In its heyday, in the early 1500s, it was a bustling place of some 200,000 people and capital of the mighty Aztec Empire. Inside Tenochtitlan, life revolved around the sacred precinct, or square, and its towering temples.

City Planning

Tenochtitlan was built in the middle of a marshy lake (Lake Texcoco) and was linked to the mainland by three huge raised-earth causeways. It was laid out on a grid pattern, divided into four quarters: the Place of Mosquitoes, the Place of the Gods, the Place of Flowers and the Place of the Herons. The city was criss-crossed by canals. Canoes were the main form of transport.

Only small areas of marshy Lake Texcoco still remain undrained.

A snake carving from the Great Temple in the sacred precinct

The Sacred Square
Dominating the city centre was the sacred precinct, with its temples, palaces, ball courts and priests' houses. It was surrounded by a wall almost 1.5 km long and only nobles were allowed inside. The most spectacular building was the Great Temple. Its twin towers were topped with two shrines, dedicated to Huitzilopochtli, god of the Sun and of war, and to Tlaloc, god of rain.

Huitzilopochtli sometimes became a hummingbird. As a result, he had a twittering bird-like voice.

Sun and Sacrifice

The Aztecs believed that the Sun died every night and was born again every morning. To make sure that the Sun rose, they offered sacrifices of human hearts and blood to the gods. In Tenochtitlan these sacrifices took place on a platform outside Huitzilopochtli's shrine. The victims' skulls were later displayed on a huge skull rack. However grisly it seems to us today, this was considered a very honourable way to die.

This is the legend of how the Aztecs founded the great city of Tenochtitlan in 1325.

◆

For many years, after leaving Aztlan, the land of their ancestors, the Aztecs wandered through deserts, forests and mountains, in search of a place to live. Four priest-rulers led their procession and carried with them a statue of mighty Huitzilopochtli, god of the Sun, and the Aztecs' guide and protector. As they travelled on and on, day after day, the god spoke to the Aztecs, to give them advice about which route to take.

"Have faith and follow me," he twittered, in his bird-like voice. "I will lead you to your city. I will make you lords of the world and give you land and riches – precious stones, amethysts and emeralds, quetzal feathers, coral and gold – beyond your wildest dreams."

Eventually, the Aztecs came to the Valley of Mexico. A local king captured them and made them fight in his army. But the Aztecs were fearsome warriors. After one battle, they cut off the ears of the men they had killed and presented them to the horrified king.

In fear for his own life, the king banished the Aztecs to a rocky island in the middle of a swampy lake. And there, in that inhospitable place, they saw the sign they had long been waiting for – a huge eagle, with a snake in its beak, perched on a cactus, bearing red fruit. The eagle was an emblem of the Sun, the sacred symbol of Huitzilopochtli himself.

"This is the place," cried the god's statue. "You must build your city here."

So the Aztecs built their great city on the site chosen by the god of the Sun. At first it was just a huddle of reed huts, with a temple dedicated to Huitzilopochtli. They called their city Tenochtitlan – the place of the prickly pear cactus. But, as the god had promised, the city swiftly grew until it became the dazzling capital of a mighty empire, which stretched from east coast to west. And the Aztecs became the lords of the world, just as the Sun god had foretold.

Mecca, City of Muhammad

The city of Mecca in Saudi Arabia is the birthplace of the prophet Muhammad, the founder of Islam. In Muhammad's time, Mecca was a major centre of trade. Its merchants grew rich by trading frankincense and myrrh for gems, gold and ivory. Today, the city is the holiest city of Islam. Muslims always turn to face Mecca to pray, wherever they are in the world. Only Muslims may enter Mecca.

The Life of Muhammad

Muhammad was born in Mecca in 570CE. He became a successful merchant, but he grew unhappy with life and with the greed he saw in Mecca. He spent more and more time in prayer. One night, in a cave on Mount Hira, an angel appeared to him and began to reveal Allah's message. Muhammad returned to Mecca to preach. He told the Meccans to worship Allah, the one true god. The words he heard were later written down as the *Qur'an*, the sacred book of Islam.

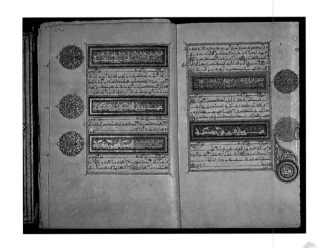

Copies of the Qur'an, *like this one, are often beautifully decorated.*

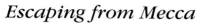

Escaping from Mecca

In 622CE, Muhammad and his followers were forced to flee from Mecca. Many of the city's rich merchants felt threatened by his preaching. On the night of 16 July, Muhammad fled to the nearby city of Medina. This journey is known as the *hijra*. It marks the beginning of the Islamic calendar. You can read the story of the *hijra* over the page. Muhammad eventually returned to Mecca in 630CE. He died in Medina in 632CE.

Pilgrims visiting Mecca walk seven times around the sacred ka'ba shrine. Muslims believe the shrine was built by Abraham.

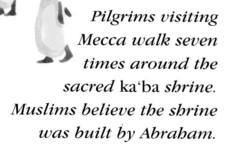

On their return home, pilgrims sometimes decorate their houses with images of the Hajj.

Journey to Mecca

Each year, millions of Muslims travel to Mecca to make a pilgrimage, called the *Hajj*, and worship at the sacred, cube-shaped *ka'ba* shrine in the centre of the city and at other sites nearby. All Muslims try to make the *Hajj* at least once in their lifetimes. It is one of the five "pillars", or duties, of Islam.

Flight to Medina

This is the story of the hijra, *the night on which Muhammad escaped from Mecca and fled to Medina.*

◆

For many years, the Prophet Muhammad lived in Mecca, the city of his birth. It was here that he heard the word of Allah and here that he started to preach the message Allah had entrusted to him. Many people listened eagerly and became Muhammad's followers. But he also gained many enemies among the city's merchants. Afraid of losing their own position and power, they persecuted Muhammad's followers and plotted to kill Muhammad himself.

On a chosen night, a group of hired men set out for Muhammad's house. But Muhammad had been warned by the Angel Jibril not to sleep at home that night. When the would-be murderers burst into his house, knives gleaming and at the ready, the man they found was not the Prophet, but his cousin, Ali.

Meanwhile, Muhammad hurried to the home of his friend, Abu Bakr, who had two sturdy camels waiting. There was no time to lose. They mounted the camels and set off for the city of Medina, and safety. But, to confuse the enemies they knew would follow, they went by a very roundabout route, so their tracks criss-crossed across the desert sand. When they reached a cool, quiet cave in the mountains, they stopped and hid.

Sure enough, Muhammad's enemies were not far behind. Furious at being tricked, the merchants offered a reward of one hundred camels to anyone who captured the Prophet. Even though the tracks confused them, they soon drew near to the cave.

"Whatever shall we do?" said Abu Bakr. "If they find us, they are bound to kill us."

"Allah will protect us," Muhammad told his friend.

And so he did. Even though their enemies found the entrance to the cave, they didn't come inside.

"There's no one there," they muttered. "Look at that spider's web right across the entrance, and that bird's nest on the ledge. No one's been here for years." Then they rode away. Allah had kept the two men hidden.

A few days later, when at last it was safe to leave the cave, Muhammad and his friend made their way across the desert to Medina, and a very warm welcome.

Footsteps of the Buddha

Bodh Gaya

INDIA

Some 2,500 years ago, an Indian nobleman, Siddhartha Gautama, arrived in Bodh Gaya, in north-eastern India. It was there that he became the Buddha – the enlightened or awakened one. Since then, his teachings have touched the lives of millions of people all over the world. And Bodh Gaya has grown from a small, sleepy village to the most revered city of Buddhism.

Life of the Buddha

Born in about 480BCE, Siddhartha Gautama grew up in his father's luxurious palace. One day, he saw four sights which changed his life – an old man, a sick man, a dead man and a monk. He decided to leave home and live like a monk, and to find the reason for the unhappiness he had seen. For six years, he lived a life of great hardship. But he did not find the answers he sought.

The Mahabodhi Temple

Gaining Enlightenment

In desperation, Siddhartha Gautama made his way to Bodh Gaya. He sat down under a spreading bodhi (fig) tree and began to meditate. That night, he gained the knowledge he had long been seeking – the true meaning of life – and so became the Buddha. Each year, thousands of pilgrims flock to Bodh Gaya. The focus of their journey is the sacred Mahabodhi Temple, with its towering spire and golden statue of the Buddha. A bodhi tree growing nearby is said to be descended from the very tree under which Siddhartha sat to meditate.

Rather than statues, many symbols are used to show the Buddha. This one is his footprint, which it is said he left at Bodh Gaya.

This is the story of how the Buddha came to Bodh Gaya and discovered the true meaning of life

◆

For six long years, after leaving his father's palace, Siddhartha lived in the forest, trying to find the meaning of life. He ate just one grain of rice a day, and slept on a bed of thorns. He grew so thin he nearly died but he did not discover the truth.

Hungry, tired and full of despair, Siddhartha left the forest behind. He wandered aimlessly until he found himself near a small, sleepy village. It was called Bodh Gaya. Here he had a nourishing meal, then he sat down beneath a spreading tree to meditate.

"I will not move from this spot until I know the answer," Siddhartha vowed.

As it got dark, the terrible demon, Mara, the evil one, appeared before him. "Why are you bothering with all of this?" Mara sneered. "Go home to your palace. Don't you miss all that good food and fine living?"

But Siddhartha did not listen – he could not go back now. All night he sat there. His mind became clear, and he felt great peace and joy. Then he began to think about the meaning of life. Why was there so much suffering in people's lives? Did they bring it on themselves? And what could they do to make things better?

In the early hours of the morning, when the world was still and the full moon shone, Siddhartha at last found the answer. The reason people suffered so much was because they were never content with what they had. They always wanted more and more. But he also saw a way out of this unhappiness. For another 49 nights and 49 days, he sat beneath the spreading tree, thinking over what he knew. From that time on, he became the Buddha, or enlightened one. The Buddha spent the rest of his life travelling far and wide through India, teaching people what he had discovered. He taught people to follow the Middle Path, a path midway between the two extremes of hardship and luxury. Then they could overcome greed and desire, and lead wiser, happier and more caring lives.

Gate of the Gods

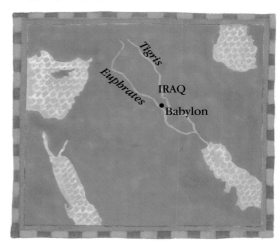

The most magnificent city in the ancient world, Babylon was the capital of a vast empire. The city stood on the banks of the River Euphrates in modern-day Iraq. This helped the city to prosper as a major trading centre. It was also a flourishing religious centre, and the name Babylon means "gate of the gods".

Hanging Gardens

The most famous place in ancient Babylon was the Hanging Gardens – one of the seven wonders of the world. According to legend, these were built by Amytis, wife of King Nebuchadnezzar II (605-562BCE). She missed the hills of her homeland so much that she created her own terraced hill next to the royal palace and covered it with exotic plants and flowers.

Rebuilding a City

King Nebuchadnezzar II was a powerful king. During his reign, Babylon was rebuilt in grand style. He built enormous city walls almost 26 metres thick, with eight bronze gates. The grandest was the great Ishtar Gate, which was decorated with bright blue tiles, lions, bulls and dragons. The Gate led to the Processional Way and the Temple of Marduk, the chief god of the city. King Nebuchadnezzar's fabulous palace stood between the Ishtar Gate and the river.

One of the bulls that decorated the Ishtar Gate.

New Year Festival

At New Year, a splendid festival was held in Babylon in honour of Marduk. It lasted for 11 days. On the fourth day, the priests recited a long poem telling how Marduk saved the world (see next page). On the last day, a great statue of Marduk was carried down the Processional Way, with great pomp and ceremony, to a temple outside the city.

*This is the story of how Marduk saved the world from chaos. This story
was recited at the New Year Festival in Babylon.*

◆

In the very beginning of the world, there was nothing but Apsu, the ocean,
and Tiamat, the sea. Their waters mixed and mingled together, and
from them came many new gods, including the great gods, Anu,
the sky god, and Ea, god of wisdom. And the first-born son of
Ea was Marduk, the great god of Babylon. Ea realised that
Marduk was perfect – he would be the lord of all
time and praised as the god of all gods.

Apsu feared the new gods. "We must destroy
them," he told Tiamat, "before they destroy us."

But Ea learned about Apsu's plan and
used his magic to kill him. And
when Tiamat discovered that her
husband was dead, she wept,
wailed and cursed. She turned
herself into a great dragon,
spitting out white-hot fire, and,
gathering an army of monsters
around her, she threatened to
destroy the world. Many times
the gods tried to beat Tiamat
back, and many times they
failed. If they were to avoid
disaster and chaos, there was
only one thing left to do.

The gods met in council. "We must call on Marduk, Ea's son," they all agreed. "He is the only one who can save us now."
So the gods summoned Marduk and made him their king, and he rode his chariot into battle against Tiamat. In his right hand, he carried his great bow and net; in his left, he held the power to summon lightning and hurricanes.

A great battle raged across the sky. Then, at its height, Marduk struck. He shot an arrow straight into Tiamat's heart, then he sliced her body in two like a fish. From one half he made the arch of the sky; the other he filled with mountains. He fixed the stars in the sky and divided the year into days. And from the blood and bones of her monstrous army he made a new creature – "I shall call it Man," he said. And so Marduk restored order to the world, with his triumph over chaos. In his honour, the gods built a temple on a huge, stepped tower in Marduk's own city, Babylon, and the people he created lived there. And every year, the Babylonians remembered Marduk's bravery on their behalf and celebrated his victory.

The Holy City

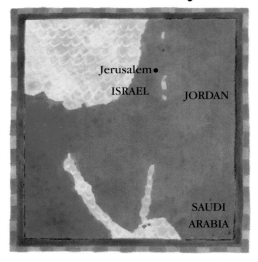

The ancient city of Jerusalem in Israel is one of the world's holiest cities, sacred to Jews, Muslims and Christians alike. For Jews, it is the ancient capital of the Jewish "Promised Land". For Muslims, it is the place where Muhammad rose into heaven. For Christians, it is the site of Christ's crucifixion and of his last days on Earth.

In the Footsteps of Christ

For Christians, the most sacred place in Jerusalem is the Church of the Holy Sepulchre. According to tradition, this was built on the site of Christ's tomb, a rock cave where he was buried and rose from the dead. A chapel inside the church contains the stone which blocked the entrance of his tomb.

This is thought to be the entrance to Christ's tomb.

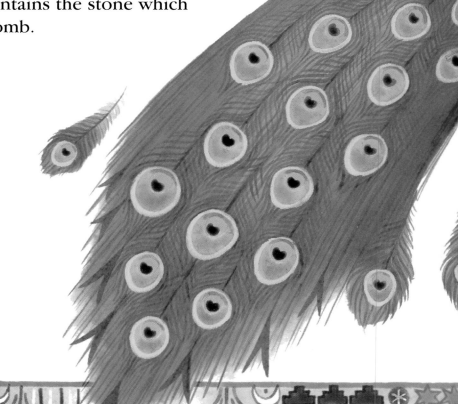

The Dome of the Rock

After Mecca and Medina (see pages 14 to 17), the mosque called the Dome of the Rock is the third holiest place in Islam. Muslims believe that Muhammad came from Mecca to Jerusalem on a strange flying beast, called Lightning, with a woman's face and a peacock's tail. He prayed at the sacred rock, then rode up to heaven where Allah taught him how to pray. The mosque now houses the rock.

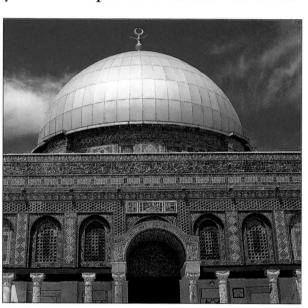

The mosque of the Dome of the Rock was built between 687and 691CE.

The Temple Mount

In about 1000BCE, David, King of the Jews, conquered Jerusalem and made it his capital. Here he brought the Ark of the Covenant, a chest containing the stone tablets on which the Ten Commandments were written. When he died, his son, Solomon, built the first Temple on Temple Mount to house the Ark.

Solomon's Temple was destroyed by the Babylonians in the 6th century BCE, rebuilt by King Herod in 31BCE, then destroyed by the Romans in 70CE. The only part of the Temple left standing is part of the wall. Known as the Western Wall, it is the Jews' most sacred shrine.

This is the story of how King Solomon built the First Temple of Jerusalem. The story comes from the Old Testament of the Bible.

Long, long ago, there lived a king who was just and wise. His name was Solomon. Under his rule, Israel grew prosperous. Solomon was famous for many great deeds. But one of the greatest, and best remembered, was the building of the Temple in Jerusalem.

When King Solomon had ruled for four years, he began to build his temple to the Lord. It was 20 cubits (11 metres) wide by 60 cubits (30 metres) long. At the front was a porch, with two tall bronze columns on either side, and inside were a great many rooms and chambers. The temple was built of finest limestone, cut and carved in a land far away, for the king did not want the sound of the hammers, or axes, or chisels to disturb the peace and quiet of the Temple. The walls, floors and ceilings were made of rich brown cedar wood, and the floors were covered with planks of sweet-smelling pine.

Then King Solomon covered the whole of the Temple in pure, glistening gold, including the altar in the Holy of Holies, the Temple's most sacred place. There the King placed two great angels carved of gold and olive wood, and each standing 5 metres tall. They stood so close

together that their gleaming wings curved over and touched in the middle of the room.

The walls and doors of the Temple were carved with angels and palms trees, and all of these were covered with gold. Indeed, everything else in the Temple was also made of gold – the candlesticks, lamps, bowls, basins and spoons, even the hinges of the doors. It was the most beautiful sight that had ever been seen.

The Temple took seven long years to build. When it was finished, King Solomon summoned all the elders of Israel and gathered together all the heads of the tribes, to bring the sacred Ark of the Covenant to the Temple. The priests placed the Ark in the Holy of Holies, beneath the curve of the golden angels' wings.

Then Solomon blessed the Temple and all the people gathered before him, raising his hands towards heaven in prayer: "I have built a house for the Lord to live in, a place for the Ark to rest for ever. May this Temple be blessed and all who worship there."

Then twenty two thousand oxen were sacrificed and a hundred and twenty thousand sheep. And, that night, a mighty feast began which lasted for seven whole days and nights, during which time there was great rejoicing among the people of Jerusalem.

Notes and Explanations

Who's Who

ATHENA: The Ancient Greek goddess of wisdom and war. In myth, she created the olive tree and gave it to the Greeks, who named the city of Athens after her in return.

AZTECS: From the 13th to the early 16th centuries, the Aztecs ruled an empire which covered much of Mexico. Their civilisation was destroyed by Spanish invaders. Their gods included the wind, the rain and the Sun, to whom they sacrificed human hearts and blood.

BABYLONIANS: The people of Babylon and its empire located in an area now part of Iraq. Babylonia existed in various forms from around 3000BCE to the 539CE, when it fell to the Persians. Babylonian civilisation influenced later Hebrew and Greek cultures.

BUDDHA: A title meaning "enlightened one" or "awakened one", given to the Indian nobleman, Siddhartha Gautama, who lived in the 5th century BCE. He sought to find a way out of life's sufferings. Millions of people still follow his teachings.

CHRISTIANS: Followers of Jesus Christ, a teacher and preacher who lived 2,000 years ago in Palestine. He was sentenced to death for his beliefs and crucified on a cross outside the city of Jerusalem. Christians believe he is the son of God. Their holy book is the Bible.

JEWS: The Jewish religion began some 4,000 years ago in the Middle East. According to Jewish law, anyone whose mother is Jewish is a Jew. There are about 14 million Jews living all over the world. Many Jews actively follow Judaism as a religion, though not all. The holy book of the Jews is the Torah.

MUHAMMAD: The last prophet of Islam, chosen by Allah (God) to carry his message to the people of Arabia. Muhammad was born in Mecca in about 570CE. He died in Medina in 632CE.

MUSLIMS: People who follow the religion of Islam, as revealed by Allah (God) through Muhammad. There are about 970 million Muslims in the world. Their sacred book is called the *Qur'an*.

What's What

Strictly speaking, fables, legends and myths are all slightly different. But the three terms are often used to mean the same thing – a symbolic story or a story with a message.

FABLE: A short story, not based on fact, which often has animals as its central characters and a strong moral lesson to teach.

LEGEND: An ancient, traditional story based on supposed historical figures or events. Many legends are based on myths.

MYTH: A story which is not based in historical fact but which uses supernatural characters to explain natural phenomena, such as the weather, seasons, night and day and so on. Ancient people used myths to understand the world around them.

COVENANT: In Judaism, a solemn agreement between God and people. God promised to look after the Jews and their descendants. The Jews promised to worship God.

MEDITATE: To concentrate and focus your mind so that you can think clearly and calmly and achieve inner peace.

NOMADIC: People who are nomadic do not live in one, settled place. Instead, they wander from place to place, in search of food and water for themselves and their animals.

PILGRIMAGE: A special journey to a sacred place as an act of religious faith and devotion. Sacred places include cities and other places connected with events in the history of a religion.

PROPHET: A person who is chosen by God to speak on God's behalf and to teach people about God's message to them.

SACRIFICE: An offering made to God, or the gods, to ask or give thanks for a favour. The Aztecs offered human sacrifices to their gods. The Greeks and Romans sacrificed animals.

Where's Where

The map below shows where in the world the places named in this book are found.

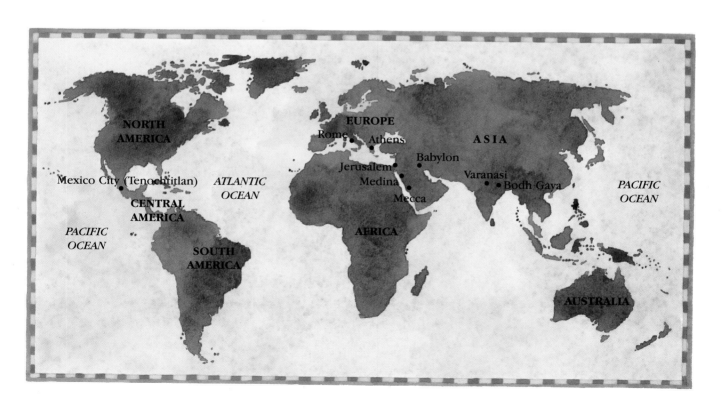

Index